Python Programming for Beginners

Learn the Fundamentals of Python in 7 Days

By Michael Knapp

Table of Contents

INTRODUCTION:

Welcome to this training for the Kindle book *Python Programming for Beginners: Learn the Fundamentals of Python in 7 Days.*

Through this book, you are going to learn everything you need to know in order to start using Python in a way that is going to make your work more productive and valuable.

Knowing how to use Python is not something that is going to be required for all jobs, but if you are looking for an ethical hacking job, a technical job, or a programming job, it is expected because Python is one of the most used programming languages out there due to the fact that it is user-friendly and it uses dynamic typing. When you have Python under your belt, you are making yourself a valuable asset to any company that is going to hire you which will put you ahead of the other applicants that do not know Python.

There is a wide variation of uses for Python, and it is hard to get away from Python in your everyday life due to the fact that it is written into almost everything that we touch. Even the kindle book that you are currently reading!

If you have used any other programming language, you are going to know some of the basics that you are going to use in Python, however, do not assume that because you know how to write out code with programs such as JavaScript that you are going to be able to write out code with Python.

There is a JavaScript version of Python that will work with JavaScript, but most versions of Python are not going to be anything similar to the other programming languages. Python is its own programming language that works off of its own rules that you are going to learn in this book!

When you go to the Python website, you are going to discover that there are several different versions that you are going to be able to download. You are going to want to go with the version of Python that is going to be the most up to date. However, some of the code that you are going to be working with is not going to work with every version of Python. This is why Python allows for you to be able to download the other versions and run your code on them without compromising the other versions of Python that are on your computer. Therefore, if you have version 2 and 3 on your PC, you are going to be allowed to work off of both of them without worrying about having to uninstall the other version when you are not using it. Pretty neat huh?

Another great thing about Python is that they are going to offer you any help that you could possibly need! If you log into their website, you are going to have the option of find forms and guides that are going to be written by a Python user just like you which are meant to help explain what you want to do in a way that hopefully, you are able to understand. Sometimes looking at the technical guides that you can import on Python are not going to be that helpful.

Should you not be able to understand after reading someone else's explanation, then there are other ways that you are going to be able to get the support that you need to figure out the issues that you are having with Python. Python is constantly changing so you should not be ashamed if you require help with something that has switched from what you are used to. Everyone needs help!

Just because Python is complicated does not mean that you should get up the first error message that you get! Just like when you were learning how to ride a bike, get back up and do it again! You are never going to be able to figure out how to write out programs with Python if you give up the first mistake that you make.

Keep pushing on and know that you are not alone in your journey to learning Python. You are going to be able to figure it out!

Note: if you are learning how to use Python in order to hack systems, please make sure that you are getting the expressed permission of the system's administrator so that you are not doing anything illegal. The information that is written inside of this book is for educational purposes only and is not meant to promote or aid in any illegal activities that it may be used for. Keep in mind that hacking is illegal everywhere in the world, and if you are caught hacking, then you are going to be punished under the full extent of the law for that area.

Hopefully, you are learning Python in order to make your job more efficient or to make a contribution to the ever-evolving world of technology.

CHAPTER 1: SYNTAX USED IN PYTHON

The language that you use in Python is going to assist you in learning the ins and outs of the program. It is with this syntax that you are going to be armed with the proper knowledge that you need in order to write out the codes that are going to create your programs in Python.

Reverse keywords

There are thirty different reserved keywords that you are going to be using when it comes to naming variables and constants. Every reverse keyword is going to have to be written in lowercase so that you are not confusing the program and receiving an error message. It is with these reverse keywords that you are going to be informing Python of the constants that are needing to be identified and what they are going to be used for.

Python identifiers

Everything that is used in Python is going to be named by an identifier. Any word that is in the English language can be utilized as an identifier; however, you are not going to be able to apply the reverse keywords. Your identifiers can be both lower and uppercase as well as contain numbers.

A disadvantage to identifiers is that you are not going to have the option of using punctuation in your identifier. Python is also a case sensitive program, therefore using the word mat and Mat are going to be two different identifiers that you are going to have to choose from when you are working. If you use one version, you must stick to it or else you are going to be creating a new identifier.

Comments

Comments are going to be notes that you put into Python. A comment is going to be set off by a number symbol that informs Python it is to be skipped whenever your code is being executed.

Comments can be inserted anywhere in your Python code being that it is going to be ignored by Python. The purpose behind comments is to write out something that you are going to need to know about the code and changes that you have made as well as inform other programmers of what operations are being used in your script should they need to modify it.

CHAPTER 2: DATA TYPES AND VARIABLES FOUND INSIDE OF PYTHON

When it comes to thinking of the variables that are used in Python, it is best that you think of it as if it is a piece of memory that is stored inside of the program where values are going to be stored. The space that is assigned to every variable is going to be dependent upon which data type that you are using. So, when you are assigning the type to the variable, you are going to be allowed to use integers, characters, and decimals in the memory of Python.

There are at least four different data types that you are going to be working with as you are writing out your Python code. These data types are:

1. Lists
2. Dictionaries
3. Tuples
4. Strings
5. And numbers

Memory location

Just like you read, the data type is going to be used when it comes to figuring out exactly how much space is going to be needed on the interpreter for the variable that Python is storing. There is not going to be anything that you can do to change about the storing of variables because this is something that has been ingrained into the Python code and it is going to be completed automatically.

Any variable that is sized in Python is going to be sized differently just like when you create a file on your computer. The biggest difference is that Python has a spot designated in its memory for where the data needs to go unlike on your computer where you are allowed to pick where the file is going to be saved.

In the event that you are working with several data types at once, you will not be allowed to use the space that the interpreter has set aside for that data type, instead, the interpreter is going to decide what needs to happen with that interpreter and then find where it should be saved so that it can be called on later.

Assigning multiple variables inside of a single statement

As you go about creating your Python code, you will have the options of putting a different value to multiple variables to cut down on how many steps that you are going to have to do for your assignments.

Example

A= e= h= 9

As you can see, the variable of a, e, and h are all going to be assigned to the value of 9. This method is going to make your code shorter and cleaner so that you are not having to search for what you are looking for when it comes to trying to figure out what variables are assigned to which value. You have also made it to where the variables are going to be saved in a single place which gets rid of the need to hunt for them later when you are trying to find them.

Now, what happens if you want to take those same variables but you want to assign them to different values, but you do not want to do multiple steps to assign them to the variables. You can do the same thing that you just did, except you are going to separate the values that you want to attach to the variables with a comma.

Example

A, e, h = 1, 4, pear

Just like the previous example, the variables are going to be assigned to the value that is occupying the same spot that the variable occupies on the opposite side of the equals sign.

So, a is going to be assigned to 1, e to 4 and h to pear.

Now that you know that, you can assign any number of variables to any number of values as long as you have one value for every variable. If you do not have a value that is in the corresponding position, then you are going to receive an error message.

Assigning values to multiple variables

You are able to use the same assignment method when you are wanting to take an amount and place it on multiple variables. Just keep in mind that you are going to be required to have a variable that will correspond to every value that you are assigning. In the event that you do not place a value in that space, then a different variable is going to be assigned to it automatically by Python so that your code is complete and it is able to execute it as it should.

Example

3, 5, 6, 2 = a, e, I, d

Converting data types

There may come a moment in time that you realize that you have written your code with the wrong data type and you need to change it. You have one of two ways that you can make this happen. One is to delete all of your code and begin writing again with the correct data type. The other way is to use a conversion method that will enable you to change from one data type to the next. It is as simple as inserting the name of the data type that you are wanting to use like you were writing out a function instead of a data type.

Any tools that have to be used for your function are going to be provided to you by the Python program. But, it is up to you to obtain the knowledge that is needed in order to use these tools properly. Whenever a data type has been converted correctly, you are not going to have to go through and delete lines of code and hours of work. You are going to be working with the same code that you have already written out, except you will now be creating a new object that will be returned to you before you insert the value for that data type that you are wanting it to be converted to.

For data conversion, you are going to use these functions.

- Oct(x): using this function is going to convert your integer into an octal string
- Int (x [, base]): x will be converted into an integer while the base tells if x comes out as part of a string or not.
- Hex(x): your integer is going to be converted into a hexadecimal string
- Long (x [, base]): x will be converted into a long integer while the base once again tells if it is part of a string or not.
- Ord(x): a single character is going to be converted into an integer value
- Float(x): the variable x will become a floating point number
- Unichr(x) this integer is going to be turned into a Unicode character.
- Complex (real [, imag]): a complex number will be created
- Chr(x): the x integer is going to be converted into a character
- Str(x): x is going to be converted into a string
- Frozenset(s): s will be converted into a frozen set
- Repr(x): you will get a result of an expression string
- Dict(d): a dictionary is going to be created. However, the d variable has to be either key or values of tuples
- Eval(str): the string will be evaluated, and you will end up with an object.
- Set(s) the variable will be converted into a set.
- Tuple(s): s is going to become a tuple
- List(s): s is going to become a list.

CHAPTER 3: THE NUMBER DATA TYPE

The most common data type that you will probably find yourself working with is the numbers data type. Just as you learned in the last chapter, you will be able to assign values to your numbers by using the same method. However, there are lots of extra things that you are going to be able to do with the number data type that you are not going to be capable of doing with other data types.

Now, when you are working with numbers, there may come the point in time that you are going to have to delete the reference that you have created to a numbered object. You can always use the delete statement which will get rid of the numbered object that needs to be removed.

Syntax

Del var1 [, var2 [, var3 […., varN]]]

That is not the only thing that the delete statement can do though. You can also use the delete statement to delete a single object, or multiple objects at once. It is going to be as easy as separating all of the objects that you want to be deleted with a comma and ensuring that you have them written out in your delete statement.

With the numeric data type, there are going to be four different subtypes that you are going to be working with.

1. Complex numbers

Example:

8.32a

2. integers that have been signed

Example

55

3. floating point numbers

example

39.21

4. long integers that have hexadecimal or octal persuasions

example

-21485731a

As you are working with the number data types, then you will need to keep something in mind so that you are not getting an error code.

1. Complex numbers are always going to be an ordered pair that is going to be created by using floating point numbers so that you can denote where the real numbers are since you are not only working with real numbers but imaginary numbers as well.

2. Long numbers are going to use a lowercase in order to inform Python as to what you are trying to do. However, you should not use this method often since a lowercase l will often times look like a one and can end up confusing the program. Instead, use an uppercase l that way it cannot be confused with anything else that you have placed into the program.

Arithmetic operators

Just like Python, math is everywhere! Just because we do not see it does not mean that it is there. Look at your phone; the chances are that it is doing math right now. Can you see it? Probably not, but does that mean it is not happening? Not necessarily. Things that we use in our everyday lives are going to use math due to the fact that it is written into the code that is causing that application to run. Python is not any different; there are codes written into the Python program that are going to take the simplest of math problems all the way up to the most complex math problem that you can think about and give you the assistance that you need to solve that problem.

Not good at math? Do not worry! You are not going to have to do any of the calculations to get the answer that you need. The only thing that you must do is insert that equation into the program so that Python does the math for you. While you are not going to have to do the calculations, you do need to ensure that you are putting the correct information into Python so that you are getting the proper results. Should you get the wrong answer, go back and look at what you put into your program, you may find your mistake and be able to fix it so that you can get the right answer.

There are some pretty standard operators that you are going to be able to use in Python, and here they are.

- Addition (+)
- The square root (math. sqrt)
- Subtraction (-)

- Exponent (b**n)
- Multiplication (*)
- Absolute value (abs ())
- Division (/)
- Negation (- x)
- Floor division (//)
- Modulo (%)

Whenever you are using the square root function in Python, you are going to need to load your math module first. To do this, you will need to go to the top of the file that you are using and insert the math module code so that it is opened and ready to be used

Python does have its downside to math though. Whenever you are using floating point numbers in your math, you may end up experiencing an error message as you attempt to round the figures after doing division. An example would be 4.0 / 2.0. You will get the correct answer, however, whenever floor division is done, you may end up getting a number that does not make any sense for the equation that has been entered.

In version 2 of Python, floor division was first introduced as a simpler way to deal with integers and longs. But, true division is going to be used whenever you are working with float and complex numbers. However, do not be shocked if you get an unexpected result. Whenever Python updated to version 3, the use of true division was made to where it can be utilized on any number you insert into the program but, do not be surprised if you still run into a few issues. This is to be expected when you are working with a program that is always updating to accommodate the needs of its users.

There is a fix though! When you are using division, place a set of parentheses around your division sign so that you get the correct answer whenever the rounding occurs inside of the program.

One last thing that you should remember about how math works in Python is that it works off of PEMDAS. This is a process that you most likely learned whenever you were in school. The beautiful thing is that you do not have to worry about following PEMDAS due to the fact that Python is going to do it automatically when it is executing your expression

P is parentheses, E is exponents, then comes M and D for multiplication and division, and finally A and S for addition and subtraction.

Example:

$9 + (85 - 9) * 7 / 6 - 4$

In following PEMDAS, your parentheses are going to come first.

$9 + (76) * 7 / 6 - 4$

Next would be the exponent, but there are not any in this particular expression, so we move on to multiplication.

$9 + 532 / 6 - 4$

Division

$9 + 88.6 - 4$

Addition

$97.6 - 4$

Subtraction

93.6

Looking at the equation written out step by step, it appears to be long and complicated, but you are going to get the proper answer. And, you are not going to have to do this process again! Python will do it for you, but it is wise for you to understand what the program is doing so if you suspect that the answer is not correct, you can go back and write out the equation and do the calculations for yourself. You may discover you entered the data in the wrong way and that is why the program did not give you the answer that you were expecting.

CHAPTER 4 FUNCTIONS THAT ARE DEFINED BY THE USER

Python offers functions that are going to be set by the user of that function. It is these functions are going to have multiple declarations that will be created inside of the program by starting with a def keyword, followed by the function name. The def keyword will tell Python what the definition of your function is.

Most of the functions that you are going to use when working with Python are going to contain arguments that will be set inside of a pair of parentheses. These functions can have more than one argument attached to it as long as the argument is stored in the proper location in the code. The brackets that surround the arguments will always have to be followed by a colon so that Python can identify that you have completed that line and are about to start a new one.

After the function that you are using has been defined, then the arguments are going to set all of the specifics that need to be established for that particular block of code. A new block of code is going to be set off by an indented line.

Syntax
Def function name (argument 1, argument 2, ...):
Statement_ 1
Statement _ 2
...

The def keyword

The def keyword is going to be used when you are defining the functions that are being used. The purpose of defining a function is so that you are able to tell Python what the functionality is so the function that you are using in order to make sure that your code is being executed the way that it should be.

- Function blocks are going to start with the def keyword as was already stated. However, if you forget to use your parentheses with your arguments, you are going to end up getting an error message due to the fact that the function you are now trying to define is not part of the Python code and Python is not going to understand what you are trying to do.

- Your arguments are not the only things that can be placed between the parentheses for your function; you can also put your parameters in the parentheses as well.

- Your first statement in your function is going to be optional, which means that you are going to have the ability to create a string for your function or to use a docstring

- Any code that is placed inside of your code block has to have a colon at the end of each declaration as well as be indented the same number of times as every other line that is in that code block. If you do not do this, you will get an error message from Python stating that your block of code cannot be executed correctly.

- When a remark is returned, there will be the option for you to go back and have your comment leave the function or for the remark to go through the expression that the user has set up. Remarks that are returned are not going to have any arguments inside of them which are going to provide the same result for the user which will be none or nothing.

Syntax

Def function name (parameters):

"function docstring."

Function_ suite

Return [expression]

The way that Python was written has made it to where the settings for all parameters are going to work off of positional behavior which will tell the parameters that your function has been set up and that it needs to be carried out in the same order that you defined it.

Example

Def printace (string)

"your string has to be passed through the function."

Print string

Return

Function name

The name of the function you are using is going to be the function that Python uses to carry out your code. However, the function name can be a string or a list that has been used inside of Python. Your function's name is important whenever working with functions that are defined by the user because it is going to tell Python what needs to be done in order to ensure you are not going to get an error message due to the program not knowing what to do being that the function is not defined by Python standards.

Parameters

Parameters are your arguments that are attached to your functions. Any parameter that you use has to be passed by a reference that is created by you in your code. So, if you are wanting to change the parameter as well as what it is referring to, then you are going to have to make sure that your parameter is reflected back to the function that it is working with.

There are four different arguments that you are going to use when you are working with Python.

1. Default arguments
2. Variable length arguments
3. Keyword arguments
4. Required arguments

Required arguments are going to the arguments that pass through your function in the same order that they are defined. Python offers a broad range of arguments that you will be able to work with inside of your function. However, you are going to need to ensure that they match what you placed in your function exactly or else Python is not going to do what it is supposed to do with that parameter

Should you decide to call the function printace (), then the function is going to have to go through at least one argument so that you do not get an error message

Example

#! /usr/bin/Python

the function has been defined.

Def printace (string)

"the line that has been coded will be required to go through the function during the step."

Print string

Return;

After the code has been carried out, Python is going to tell you that you need to put at least one argument into your function since one has not been placed into your code. To fix this, you will need to return to where your parameters belong and insert there which will take care of the error message that you are receiving.

Keyword arguments are related to the functions that are being called on. In using this argument, you are going to have to identify which argument that is being employed by the name of the parameter that is being used.

You can skip over the arguments that have been placed into your function, or you can put them in any order that you are wanting to due to the fact that the interpreter is going to be able to tell which argument that needs to go next since it is going to match the keywords with their arguments.

Default arguments are going to be the arguments that are put into Python by Python since you did not put an argument into the program for the function to call on.

Depending on what Python is being used for, you may discover that you are going to need to process a function that is going to have multiple arguments attached to it. To do this, you will be using a variable length argument.

Syntax

Def function name ([formal_ args,] * var_args_tuple):

"function docstring

Function suite

Return [expression]

Whenever asterisks are seen before a variable name, the value is going to be the sum of every non-keyword argument that is found inside of your code. The tuple that you get as an outcome is going to be empty since there are not going to be any other arguments that will be defined whenever the function has been called on.

Colon

Colons are going to be used a great many ways when it comes to Python. Some things that a colon can be applied to are the slicing of indexes or to tell the program when a line has ended, and a new one is about to start. It is basically a semicolon with several other functions tied to it.

Docstring

The doc string is the string literal that will happen inside of the first line for the class or function that is being used. Docstrings will be set apart by underscores that are going to be located before and after the word doc.

Whenever you are working with modules, there has to be a doc string inside of the file that is exported by that particular module.

A string literal that is found in Python will act as if it is a document which is not going to be recognized by the bytecode that Python uses. Since it is not recognized, the string literal will not be accessible to any object that is working with runtime.

Two different types of docstrings may or may not be extracted by the software tools that are being used in Python.

1. A string literal where the assignment is to take place at the top of the module or the class which is also known as the attribute docstrings.

2. A string literal will fall after all other docstrings, and the doc strings that are written after the first line will be known as additional docstrings.

As the user of Python, you will have the choice of using triple quotes inside of the docstrings that you work with. When triple quotes are used, the docstring will be turned into a Unicode docstring. If you do not use backslashes, the program is not going to be able to confuse your docstrings with other objects that are being worked on in Python.

There is also the option of writing docstrings that span across multiple lines. These are typically going to work as a single line doc string, but after you have completed the typing that is required for that docstring, there is going to be a blank line that is inserted which will then be followed by a description of the code that has just been written.

Summary lines are going to be used whenever you are using the automatic indexing tools. These summer lines have to be placed on a single line to ensure that it does not get mixed in with the rest of the docstring that you have just created.

The summary line will be the line that the open quote is located on or it can be found on the one that follows it. All docstrings will have to be indented the same amount of times and use the exact same quotes. So, if single quotes are used at the beginning of the line, they have to be used at the end of the line. This is going to make your code look presentable, and you are not going to have to spend a bunch of time attempting to find something that may need to be fixed in your code whenever you get an error message from Python.

CHAPTER 5: PYTHON LISTS

Lists are one of the most fundamental data structures that are used in Python. Any element that is put inside of a list is going to have a number assigned to it so that there is an element for it in your index. The index is always going to start at zero and move forward.

There are at least six difference sequences that have been built into Python so that they can be used when you are writing out your code. However, the ones that you are going to see most often are the list and the tuples.

When working with sequences, the tools that you need in order to slice indexes, insert multiple objects, and check for membership will be provided to you through code in Python. You are going to have the option of using functions that are built into Python so you can discover how long the sequence is and locate the largest and smallest items in that series.

Creating lists

In order to create a list, you are going to simply insert the elements that you want inside of that list inside a set of square brackets followed by a comma after each item. You do not have to stick to just one data type in your list because lists are versatile and are able to handle a wide variety of data types in one list.

Example

List z = [' books', '4', 'television', '2']

Accessing list elements

Whenever you are working with a list, you are going to need to try and avoid calling it a list whenever it comes to defining the function. When you do this for every list that you work within Python, you are going to run into the very real possibility that you are going to end up confusing your lists with other lists that you have created which will then cause your code to not the work that it is supposed to because you are working with list elements that are not meant to be inserted into the code that you are working with. This is why you are going to want to give each list a unique name.

In accessing the elements in your list, you will need to make sure that you have access to print your index. Please keep in mind that when accessing elements you need to be able to access where that index starts and where it ends. However, when it comes to creating that index, you are going to be going one element past where you want the index to end so that all the items are included in your index.

Example print (catdog [3] [4], list dogcat [3] [5])

Adding elements to a list

Sometimes elements are going to need to be added to your list because they were forgotten or because you want to discover how a code will work with a different set of elements in the list. This is when you are going to want to update your list so that there are new elements on your list.

Example

```
#! / usr/ bin/ Python
List a= ['books', 'CDs, 568, 985];
Print "the value that is located at the third index."
Print lis [a]
List [a] 985
Print "add new value to the second index."
Print list [a]
Result
Your previous value was 568
Your new value is 42.
```

Element changes

Updates are not always what needs to happen when it comes to modifying your list. There will be times that you should need to replace elements completely. In your attempt to do this, you are going to need to identify the position of the element and what that element needs to be changed to.

Example

```
List z = [ a, b, c]
List z [2]
List z [2] = h
List z
[a, b, h]
```

Concatenating and repeating

Two lists can be added together when you are using Python, and you will be using the same method that is used whenever you are working with strings. First, you should ensure that both lists are listed before you place a plus sign between them which will be what tells the program that you are wanting them to be added together.

Example

List 5 = list 1 + list 6

Result

List 5 now has every element from list 1 and list 6.

Some items will need to be repeated in Python and to do this you are going to be allowed to pick one of two methods that Python has to offer as you are creating your code. One method is the long method, and the other method is going to be the shorter method which is preferred because your code is going to be cleaner in the event that you need to modify it.

Method one: a number of times in xrange(d)

Method two: [a] * d

In this example, you are going to be assuming that the variable that has to be repeated needs to be repeated not in one list, but in two different lists and the number of variables that have to be repeated is going to be different for each list.

31

Example

[m] * 4

M, m, m, m

[m] * 3

M, m, m

Removing elements

When you are taking elements off a list, there are going to be two methods that you are going to be able to use. First is the del statement which should only be used when you have to delete a specific element that should be removed from your list. The remove technique, on the other hand, is going to be used when all the elements need to be taken off your list.

Example

List a = ['title', 'name', 'animal',]

Print list a

Del list a [1]

Print everything that falls after the first index

Print list a

Result

List a ['title', 'name']

Sort

The sort method can be used for any element that you find on your list. You are not going to be using the function method, but the sort method is going to sort method will work similarly to this method.

Syntax:

List. Sort([func])

The function that is being used in the example that follows will not have any parameters.

Example

```
#! / usr/ bin/ Python

A list= [46, apple, moon, lie, flea];

A list.sort()

Print list
```

Result

A list [46, apple flea lie moon];

The count () method

With the count method, you are going to be able to get a result of how many times something is listed in the list that you are working with.

Syntax

List. Count(obj)

You are going to have to follow the parameters that are set into place for this method though, and that parameter will be the object parameter. It is this parameter that is going to give you the answer as to how many times objects are found on the list that you are currently working with.

Example

#! / usr/ bin/Python

Zlist = [46, apple flea lie moon, moon, moon]

Print "number of times moon appears zlist. count (moon)

Result: number for moon: 3

CHAPTER 6: TUPLES AND THEIR USES IN PYTHON

A tuple is also a sequence that is going to contain objects that do not have the ability to be modified which causes a tuple to be an immutable data type. Tuples will look similar to the list, but some differences cause them to be two different data types. The biggest discrepancy that you are going to notice right off the bat is that the tuple will not be seen inside of a set of square brackets. Rather, a tuple will be using a set of parentheses. While this is a small difference, it is going to be the difference of having your code executed correctly by Python.

Creating tuples

Tuples are going to be set up through the use of making a list of elements by separating them by commas inside of a set of parentheses. The parentheses do not have to be used if you do not want to or you happen to forget. The parentheses are there to make your code look more presentable.

Example

Tup a = ('television,' 'radio, 'books,' 'CDs)

Tup b = s, t, u, v, w

Tuples that are empty can also be placed inside of the code

that you are working with and the way you do this is the same way as when you create a tuple, the only difference will be that you are not going to be put anything between the parentheses but a simple space. This is what will cause an empty tuple to be returned. The same method can be used when you want a single element to be inside of your tuple.

Accessing tuple elements

Elements that are in your tuple can be accessed by using a set of square brackets as if you were trying to cut the index due to the fact that this is going to be exactly what you are doing.

Example

```
#! /usr/bin/Python

Tup a = ('television,' 'radio,' 'books,' 'Xbox')

Tup b = a, m, n, e, z

Print tup a [1], tup a [1]

Print tup b [2:4], tup b [2:4]

Result

Tup a: television

Tup b: m, n
```

Indexing

Since tuples are sequences, you are going to have an index that goes along with that tuple. The index is going to inform you of where all of the elements are inside of said tuple. This index can be used when you need to splice the tuple so that you can create a new tuple or so that you can get access to the elements that you have listed in your tuple.

Example

Tup a = ('television,' 'radio,' 'books,' 'Xbox')

Television is on index zero since that is where the index is always going to start.

Radio is on 1

Books on 2

And Xbox on 3

At any point in time that you are needing to access elements, you are going to have to declare where the access point starts and where it ends. Just like when you are creating an index, you are going to have to go one element past where the last one is going to be located. This is done due to how Python is written, and there is nothing that you are going to be able to do about it. So, if you want to ensure that you include all of the right elements in your index, you will need to do this, or else your program may not run the way that you want it to run.

Negative indexing

Negative indexes are the exact same as a regular index,

except you are working with negative numbers obviously. When you are using a negative index, you will be starting with the number that is at the end of the list first and then moving backward.

Example

```
D = [ 3, 8. 6]
Print d [-6]
1
Print d [-8]
2
print d [-3]
3
```

Slicing tuples

Tuples can be sliced in the exact same manner that an index is sliced. Whenever a tuple is sliced, a new tuple is created with identical objects inside of it that are going to be transferred from the original tuple.

Example

Tup 2 = [5, 2, 9, 4, 8, 2, 0, 4, 7]

2[2:6]

Result

9, 4, 8, 2, 0, 4

Reassignment and deletion

Tuples are immutable remember!

With that being said, if you have made a mistake in what is

entered in your tuple or you are seeking a way to modify an error, then you are going to have to delete the entire tuple and restart with a new one. When you have to do this, you will want to double check every item that is in your tuple to make sure that you want it to be there before you put it into the program or else you are going to have the same issue occur and once again will have to go through the steps of deleting and recreating the tuple properly.

Whenever tuples have to be deleted, you can delete it in one step by using the del statement. This is going to erase every trace of the tuple that was in your program ensuring that you do not have any piece of it left behind to give you issues later.

Example

#! /usr/bin/Python

Tup 2 = [5, 2, 9, 4, 8, 2, 0, 4, 7]

Print tup

Del tup;

Print "your tuple is gone"

Print tup

After you have used the del statement, you are not going to have any tuple left to be returned or defined. If you end up getting an error message, this is okay because you have already gotten rid of the tuple that was giving you issues.

Here is where you will be able to create a new tuple that contains all of the right elements!

CHAPTER 7: STRINGS

Strings are another one of the most commonly used data types in Python. When you are creating a string, you will have to put all of the characters that you want into the string inside a set of quotation marks. The same rules that you have to abide by when you are assigning values is going to apply here as well.

String characters

When it comes to creating strings, the characters in your strings are going to be able to be letters or they can be numbers. Strings in all reality are not a complex data type to work with; in fact, they are one of the easiest that you are going to have the chance to work with because of how simple they are.

Example:

Variable 1 = "you have created a string."

Variable 2: "variable 2 [8]

Despite the fact that there are multiple data types used in the example above, the two examples show just what a string is going to look like.

Strings also come with escape characters. These characters will be the characters that Python is unable to print unless they first have a backslash placed in front of them. When you use an escaped character, your Python interpreter has to take the character and then print it into the character string inside of a set of quotes.

The escaped characters are:

- \xnn: this is a hexadecimal notation that says the variable of n falls between 0 and 9 as well as a to f or even A to F
- \a: a bell or alert
- \x: the character of x
- \b: backspace
- \v: a vertical tab
- \cx: control-x
- \C-x: control-x
- \t: a regular tab
- \e: escape
- \s: space
- \f: form feed
- \r: carriage return
- \M- \C-x: a meta-control-x
- \nnn: an octal notation where your n value will fall between 0 and 7
- \n: start a new line

String indexing

The index for your string is going to come from the str function that is used when you create a string or a substring. String indexes are going to be where the string starts and where it ends much like any other index in Python.

Syntax

Str.index (str, beg = 0 end = Len (string))

And, much like other indexes in Python, there are a few rules that you have to keep in mind so that you can make sure you are indexing your string properly.

1. Beg: your string index will begin here, and it is going to be set to start at zero by default.
2. End: the index is going to end here and informs you of how long your string is.
3. Str: this function is going to tell Python where part of the string is located and where it should begin its evaluation.

The index for a string is going to be in a category all by itself because there is an exception to the string index rule that is going to make it to where you cannot use the str function.

Example

#! / usr/bin/Python

String 1 = "hello there, I am a string."

String 2= "oh look, another string!"

Print string 1. Index (string 1)

Print string 1. Index (string 2, 4)

Print string 1. Index (string 2, 3)

The len () function

This function is going to operate much like the count function except that you should only use it when you are working with strings in order to figure out how long the string is. If you attempt to use the count function with a string, you are going to get an error message.

Syntax:

Len (str)

Len () is not going to have any rules that you have to follow like the str () function does. Therefore, all you need to do is include it into your code, and your answer will be revealed to you as soon as Python evaluates the string.

Example:
```
#! / usr/ bin/ Python
Str = "strings are fairly easy to understand, aren't they?"
Print len (str)
Result: 8
```

Slicing a string

Should you ever need to pull part of your code out of your string, you are going to use the slicing method that you use whenever you are slicing indexes. Just select the location in which the slice needs to begin and then where it needs to end. Just like when you are slicing an index, you are going to have to go one element further than where you would like the slice to end so that all the proper elements are being included in the slice.

Example

A [2: 9]

For this example, the slice that you have created will start at two and end at eight

Example:

"I am making a string to set an example for you."

A [2: 4]

Result: am making

String concatenating

Whenever a string is concatenated, two different strings are going to be combined in order to create a single string. You have to be careful when you are concatenating strings tough because you may discover that you connected two strings together causing your code not to make much sense to the user of the program. When two strings are added together, a string object will be created.

A plus sign is going to be the symbol that you use in order to add two strings together through the interpreter.

Example

Str 1: "This string."

Str 2: "and this string are going to become one."

Str 1 + str 2

Result

"This string and this string are going to become one.

Sadly, Python is not programmed to be able to combined strings that contain both integers and characters due to the fact that they are two different data types. Therefore, if you are wanting to connect a string that has integers, you are going to have to convert that integer into a string so that you are able to combine them.

Example

Print 'pink +'purple.'

Pinkpurple

Print 'blue' * 2

Blueblue

Print 'blue' + 5

Error: Strings and integers cannot be concatenated

As you look at the example above, you will see that the character can be multiplied by a number to give you the same character printed out twice. However, in an attempt to add them together, you will get an error message since what you are trying to do is going to be considered a mathematical equation by Python. While the multiplication should be considered an equation as well, Python allows for this to happen. No one quite understands why it is just one of the things that the programmers decided to do when they were writing out the code for Python.

Being that strings are stored in the Python memory bank, you can record any character that has been used before into a string. When you want to work with integers that are not going to be decimals, it will be stored as a numbered value. However, since Python is considered to be an advanced piece of technology, it is still not able to combine words and integers as we just discussed. This is the reason as to why integers will need to be converted before they can be coupled with another string.

When you are doing the actual converting of an integer, you will be using the str method!

The str () method

Str is going to be the function that is used whenever a new string needs to be created. It is one of the functions where anything that is listed inside of the parentheses will be made into a string. Therefore, make sure you are placing every element you want in your string in between these parentheses along with surrounding them with quotations marks. You are going to do this in an effort to set it aside from other Python codes so it can be executed properly.

Example

Str 1 = 'This string is located inside a set of single quotes.'

str 2= "This one is located inside a set of double quotes."

CHAPTER 8: PYTHON LOOPS

Many times, Python is going to execute a statement in the order that they appear in Python. This means that Python is not going to jump around in the code executing different parts of the code. Instead, it will start at the beginning and work from there. But, do not be surprised if you end up having to run a block of code multiple times over in an effort to get the results that you need.

A vast majority of programming languages that are available for you to learn will offer you some sort of control when it comes to the manipulation of execution paths that may be difficult to work with.

Loop marks are going to be how you can carry out you statements multiple times in a row without the need to write the same statement over and over again.

'for' loops

'For' loops enable items to be iterated as long as they are listed in the sequence you are working with. This means you can work with lists and strings in your 'for' loop.

Syntax

For iterating_var in sequence:

Statements(s)

In the event that your sequence is part of an expression list, then it is going to have to be evaluated before it can be executed. You cannot work around this; it is another thing that no one but the developers of Python understands.

After it has been evaluated and located in your sequence, a value will be assigned to it so that it can be iterated. It is from this point on that each statement is going to have a value assigned to it before it is carried out up until each remark found in Python has been evaluated and executed. There may be a few statements that end up being run through a few times just to make sure that the iteration is complete and no statement has been skipped over.

A second option is that you can iterate an element that is located in the list by using the index that is attached to that particular sequence.

Example

#! /usr/bin/Python

Vegetables = ['carrot', 'green bean,' 'squash']

For the index that is inside of the range (Len(vegetables));

Print 'current vegetable: ', vegetables[index]

Print "program is being terminated."

Result

Current vegetable: carrot

Current vegetable: green bean

Current vegetable: squash

Program is being terminated

As you just saw, the len () function was performed to assist in giving the correct number of elements that were in the list that was found in the tuple. It also gave the range for the elements in the function which gave the sequence to be iterated.

Python allows for the 'else' statement to be used in the event that there is a loop found in your code.

Elise statements are placed in your code whenever the loop has been moved over the entire list and performed every action that can be carried out.

Example

```
#! /usr/bin/Python

For var in range (1, 65)

For m in range (87, var)

If var m <= 87

L = var / m

Print % a equal to %a * % a

Break

Else

Print var when it is a prime number
```

'while' loop

The 'while' loops are going to always be executed within the same code block up until the condition that has been set into place is met. The result that you are going to get will either be true or false only.

Syntax

While expression:

Statement(s)

The statements located in a 'while' loop are going to be used as single remarks or a block of remarks that will be created based on what the goal you are trying to accomplish is. Any condition that you put into place for your expression that is equivalent to the result of true cannot be equal to a non-zero value. The loop is going to go up until this condition is met, even if the loop has to go on forever.

After the point in time has been reached where the condition can no longer be found as true, any pass that is sent to the loop will be controlled by Python.

As you use Python, you may realize that some remarks are going to be indented the same amount of times as other remarks. This is going to be an indication of a code block. Whenever this block is inserted into the 'while' loop, the loop will go through the entire code block until it finds a line of code that makes your condition true or false.

Whenever you get the result of false, the loop is then going to skip over that condition after Python has executed it.

Example

#! /usr/bin/Python

Count = 2

While (count >100)

Print "what the current count is."

Count = count +7

Print "program terminated."

It is inside of this example that you will take note that the statement will be increased by 7 each time that it is run up until the count is no longer greater than 100.

An infinite loop is going to contain a condition that can never be found as false. Infinite loops cannot be used too often since, as the name suggests, they are never going to end. Therefore, it will take a lot of time to watch as Python continues to run through the same section of code, again and again, no matter how many lines of code you are working with.

The only time that you will find an infinite loop to be useful is when you are working with servers and their clients. On the server side, the program is going to have to be run continuously so that it can communicate with the customer's server so that the client has constant access to the information that is required to keep the business up and going.

Example

```
#! /usr/bin/Python

Num = 5

While num == 5
```

Var = raw_input (place your number in this slot)

Print "the number that you are inputting."

Print "program terminated."

The result for the loop that is shown above is going to be a loop that never ends. So, when you want to end the program, you will need to hit Ctrl + C so that the program forces the loop to end. Whenever you open the file containing that loop once more, it will pick up and run where it left off.

Example

#! /usr/bin/Python

Count = 6

While > 987

Print count if the count is greater 30000

Count = count +5

Else print count "when the count is not greater than 30000

A single statement is going to have syntax that looks similar to your 'while' loop, however, it is only going to work with a single statement rather than a block of code. This can be helpful in the moments when the statements are placed into the header being that it is the only statement that is being put into Python, therefore, leaving all of the room that is in the body of your command prompt to be filled with other pieces of code.

Example

```
#! /usr/bin/Python

Flat = 7

While (flag) print "the statement that is placed there for the flag has to be true."

Print "program terminated."
```

It is not suggested that you attempt to run this code in Python because there is a possibility that you will end up getting an infinite loop.

Break statement

A break remark is going to be what causes loops that are currently running to be terminated so that the following code can be carried out. Should you have any experience working with C programming, you are going to understand how this statement works.

You are going to use a break because you have inserted a new condition and you need the loop to be terminated. Break remarks are not only going to work for "while" loops but "for" loops as well.

Nested loops that use a break statement will cause the innermost loop to be stopped so that the first line on the outer loop can start.

Syntax

Break

Example

#! /usr/bin/Python

For the letters that you find in Good bye

If letter == 'o'

Break

Print 'the current letter': ,' letter

Num = 2

While num > 67

Print 'the current value.'

Number = num -4

If num >= 10:

Break

Print "program closed."

CHAPTER 9: PYTHON ERRORS AND EXCEPTIONS

It is not too unusual to observe an error message pop up due to the fact that you have entered something incorrectly. Another possibility is that you have something else that is going on with Python that you may not see right away, but an error message is still going to be given to you.

Error messages are not the only messages that you can get; you can also get an exception to the rules that Python has set into place so that you are able to enter a value differently than what Python typically accepts.

Errors

The syntax error is going to be one of the most common mistakes that you are going to get when working with Python. This sort of mistakes is going to occur whenever Python does not understand one of the lines of code that has been entered. While it is one of the most frequent errors, it is also one of the most a fatal ones due to the fact that the code you are trying to execute is not going to be able to be implemented successfully when this error is given.

Some mistakes are able to be fixed even after the code has been executed. You can use the code eval ("). However, the chance of getting an error like this is very rare.

As you are working with IDLE any syntax error is going to

be located due to the fact that they are going to be highlighted for you to see in many cases, a syntax error occurs because of a typo, you did not use the correct indention, or you used the wrong argument. When you get a syntax error, you are going to need to start looking in these places first before you look anywhere else.

Logic errors are one of the hardest errors for you to find due to the fact that they are unpredictable results and can cause the program to crash. Logic errors can occur for several reasons.

Thankfully, the logic errors are going to be easy to fix due to the fact that the sole thing you have to do is run a debugger through your code so that the problems are located, and you are able to fix them in order to get the results you desire.

Exceptions

An exception happens whenever the Python program knows what needs to be done with the code, but it cannot perform that action due to an outside source that is working against the code that you have created. One of the biggest issues is going to be something such as trying to access the internet. Python does understand what you are trying to do, but an outside force is stopping it from doing what you want such as your internet router being turned off.

When you are dealing with exceptions, you are going to see that it is not like when you are working with syntax errors since they are not going to be fatal every time that you see one. An exception is going to give you the ability to be handled with a try statement.

If you look at the code that follows, you are going to see that it is being used to display the HTML that you see on your favorite web page. Whenever you are executing the program, a try statement is going to try and be reached so that the code can be performed as it has been written. However, for some reason, an error is going to be given due to the fact that your router is not connected to the internet or something similar. In this case, your interpreter is going to skip to the first line of indented code.

Import urllib5

URL = 'HTTP:// www.ababykitten.com'

try

  Req = urllib5. Request(URL)

  response = urllib5. URL open(reg)

        the page = response. red ()

              print the page

except:

        print " We have a problem"

With an exception, you may notice that the URL that you insert is going to not be able to be entered for the reason that your program discovers. When this happens, you have the option of handling the error message with an exception that is going to be set for that particular error.

Example:

Age = int (raw_input ("Enter your age: "))

Print " You must have be at least this old {0} to enter.".

Format(age)

Except for Value Error:

Print: the value for your number has to be numeric.

Any exceptions that allow for you to predict them because you are going to know what needs to be entered into the data that you are working with so that the program works the way that it is supposed to.

The other exceptions that you will run into when working with Python are going to be the ones that are still going to be easy for you to deal with, but they may not be as simple as the exception that we just discussed.

You should keep in mind that the program is going to know what it is that you are trying to do when you use an exception. However, Python is not going to be able to execute the exception due to the issue that you have to deal with. Whenever an error is displayed, you are not necessarily going to be able to fix it because it could end up being something that is beyond your control. In the event that you are not able to find the error, then you can follow a few things that are going to make it to where you can get the error. But, if it is a syntax error, you are not going to have the capabilities to fix it. When this happens, you are going to have to restart with your code so that you do not make the same mistake a second time.

CONCLUSION:

Thank you for making it through to the end of *Python Programming for Beginners: Learn the Fundamentals of Python in 7 Days*, let's hope it was informative and able to provide you with all of the accessories you need to accomplish your goals whatever it may be.

The next step is to take everything that you have learned in this book and apply it to your programming.

If you are learning Python in an attempt to get a better job that is going to help you advance and succeed, then I hope you were able to learn enough that you are in a position to make progress to the next step.

As you read in the introduction, Python offers a wide variety of uses, and if you are learning Python for hacking purposes, you need to do it legally so that you are not punished by the law. When you are hacking someone's system with their permission, it is always a good idea to get written permission from them that way that if you get caught by someone getting into a system that is not yours, you have hard proof that shows that you are not doing anything illegal.

In the event that you do not feel like this is the safest method, you can always set up a virtual environment that is going to allow you to hack into your own system as if it is a stranger's system. This may end up being the safest method for you, so do not forget about it when you are using Python for hacking.

Finally, if you found this book useful in any way, a review on Amazon is always appreciated!

Thank you and good luck on using what you have learned in this novel to work with Python. It is my hope that by learning Python you are going to be able to enhance your life in a way that makes the work that you do or are wanting to do easier.

Do not forget to look for the intermediate book that will assist you in taking what you have learned one step further!

OTHER BOOKS BY MICHAEL KNAPP

1) : Python For Beginners: Learn the Fundamentals of Python in 7 Days

2) Python For Intermediates: Learn the Fundamentals of Python in 7 Days

3) Python For Advanced: Learn the Fundamentals of Python in 7 Days

DID YOU ENJOY THIS BOOK?

I want to thank you for purchasing and reading this book. I really hope you got a lot out of it.

Can I ask a quick favor though?

If you enjoyed this book I would really appreciate it if you could leave me a positive review on Amazon.

I love getting feedback from my customers and reviews on Amazon really do make a difference. I read all my reviews and would really appreciate your thoughts.

Thanks so much.

Michael Knapp

p.s. You can <u>click here</u> to go directly to the book on Amazon and leave your review.

Made in the USA
San Bernardino, CA
28 June 2017